Copyright 2019 by Mim Hosking

Published by Tanquillity Rise (ABN 53 124 414 722)

All rights reserved. No part of this publication may be reproduced or transmitted in any form or by any means, electronic or mechanical, including photocopying, recording, storage in an information retrieval system, or otherwise, without the prior written permission of the publisher, unless specifically permitted under the Australian Copyright Act 1968 as amended.

For further information go to www.tranquillityrise.com
Illustrator: Evgeniya Erokhina www.instagram.com/artdjen
Book Design: Kellie Book Design www.facebook.com/kelliebookdesign

First Printed 2019
Printed by Ingram Spark; USA

Tranquillity Rise

There's a new baby at my place.

Mim Hosking

Illustrated by: Evgeniya Erokhina

For Austin, Zac & Mark.
Watching you grow and become family has been one of my greatest delights in life. ~ MH

For Kate.
You complete our family. ~ EE

There is a new baby at my place.
He is sleeping.

There is a new baby at my place.
She is crying.

There is a new baby at my place.
He is changing.

There is a new baby at my place.
She is drinking.

There is a new baby at my place.
He is growing.

There is a new baby at my place.
She is eating.

There is a new baby at my place.
He is bathing.

There is a new baby at my place.
She is walking.

There is no baby at my place.

He is a big boy just like me,
and together we make a family.

GOING DEEPER:

As an educator or a parent, it is valuable to encourage children to retell a story and consider the characters, setting and relate the events to their own lives. These questions may assist you in this discussion process. It is suggested that you choose two to three questions to ask children after each time you read the story or focus on one page and ask specific questions about the illustration.

DISCUSSION QUESTION IDEAS:

About the story.

* What is this story about?
* Who are the characters in this story?
* Why is there no baby at the end of this story?
* What do you notice about the baby in this story?
  (Look at how the baby is growing. Each baby belongs to a different family.)
* What things grow and change?
* Have you ever had to get used to a big change? What happened?
* What advice would you give to a child who has a new family member arriving at their place?

Focus on one page:

* Who is in this family?
* Where do you think the family live?
* What do you notice about their culture?
* How is the older child feeling in this picture? Why?

www.ingramcontent.com/pod-product-compliance
Lightning Source LLC
Chambersburg PA
CBHW041326290426

44110CB00004B/157